OVERCOMING
THE
FEAR FACTOR

THE CUT FROM CORPORATE TO CREATIVE

TENITA C. JOHNSON

Published by So It Is Written, LLC
Detroit, MI
SoItIsWritten.net

Overcoming the Fear Factor: The Cut from Corporate to Creative
Copyright © 2021 by Tenita C. Johnson

All rights reserved. No part of this book may be reproduced or transmitted in any form or by any means, electronic or mechanical, including photocopying, recording, or by an information storage and retrieval system—except by a reviewer who may quote brief passages in a review to be printed in a magazine or newspaper—without permission in writing from the publisher.

Edited by: Shairon Parks and Isabelle Stroobandt

Formatting: Ya Ya Ya Creative – www.YaYaYaCreative.com

ISBN: 978-1-7362170-2-3

LCCN: 2020924224

PRINTED AND BOUND IN THE UNITED STATES OF AMERICA

Table of Contents

Introduction 1

Get to the Root 5

The Rear-View Mirror 15

Accountability Partners 27

Plan & Practice 37

In the Shadows 49

Prayer 59

Execute 71

"F" the Fear Factor 81

About the Author 83

About So It Is Written 84

Introduction

Oftentimes, it starts with a loud boom. A bang. A startling moment. Something that catches you off guard. A thing for which you haven't had time to prepare. Suddenly, your instinct, your internal self can only resort to what your mind, body and soul experience naturally—fear.

If you attempt to get a reaction out of a newborn baby with a scary mask or horror movie, you'll probably fail tremendously. Fresh out of the womb, a baby doesn't know fear. It learns to fear. It is taught. If you see a dog charging at you and barking, your instinct is to run away from the dog. If you hear gunshots while you're walking on the street at night, your instinct is to take cover and find shelter. The local newscaster predicts severe weather or a snowstorm for the next 24 hours and, suddenly, the line at the grocery store becomes significantly longer with people stocking up on basic necessities. Though the magnitude may vary from person to person, or situation to situation, we all experience fear at some point in our lives.

Let's take my three children for example. My oldest son, who is now 23 years old and out of the house, has always been a person who doesn't show much emotion—good or bad. I've never seen him yell or scream at anyone. He didn't fall on the floor and cry when he didn't get his way as a child. He doesn't cry at funerals. He didn't even cry when he got spankings, come to think of it. On the flipside, when he received gifts for Christmas or his birthday, he was grateful, but someone needed to notify his emotions to swing into action. He'd say, "Thank you," and maybe offer a smirk. But he never jumped up and down while shouting, "Thank you so much!" even while he opened that one thing he'd asked for. But he rides roller coasters without hesitation. He studied abroad in Cape Town, South Africa for six months, went bungee jumping off a cliff and fed wild animals. Nothing seems to scare him. Nothing seems to move him to the point of drastic emotions, not one way or the other.

On the contrary, my middle child, Xavier, shakes like a leaf at the first sign of trouble. He's immediately frantic. If you walk in a room quietly, it's likely you'll startle him, and he will instinctively jump or scream. Up until the age of 13, he always requested we leave the bathroom light on at night—just in case. When he's home alone, he locks all the doors and shuts all the curtains. And while he loves Halloween because of the free candy, he always asks me to drop him off at school instead of riding the bus that particular day—as if evil and trouble is limited to just Halloween. He doesn't like when water gets in his eyes while in the shower out of fear that somehow, some way, he would drown. He also loves to ride roller coasters, but it's a process to actually get through the line and onto the ride. He asks questions while we're waiting; he has to see how the ride starts, how high it takes you and how it ends. Like me, when he sees a dog charging at him, he runs or screams. He's afraid of spiders (or any bug, for that matter), lightning and thunder, and fireworks. The level of fear in my sons is like night and day. They're on totally different ends of the "fear" spectrum.

Then, I had a girl. Nyla loves *Frozen* dolls, YouTube videos and puzzles. As one may expect, she's afraid of spiders, ants and thunder. She's been on a small roller coaster long enough to know she didn't want to get back on again. But she's not afraid of hiding in the dark, so she will jump out and actually attempt to scare *you*. She's not afraid to put her head underwater at the water park and she can often be found jumping from the bed (or the bathroom sink) onto the floor. While she does show some level of fear, I'm convinced that she is on a mission to create fear in others. In some sick way, she finds it quite funny when others are scared because of something she has done.

Just like my children, everyone has varying levels of fear. It's the internal alarm that sounds within us, saying,

"Something is wrong." It's the fight-or-flight response. If you don't want to fight, or you feel like you won't win the fight, you may opt for flight. Nonetheless, we all have some level of fear. But what I've learned about fear over time is that it grips you.

It stops you. It brings everything to a halt, for many. Many people don't fly because they are scared the plane may fall out of the sky. Others don't start businesses, write books or open that clothing store because they fear failure. Some people won't go into certain neighborhoods because they fear they may get shot. But, if we accomplish nothing more, I hope by the time you complete this book, you will have conquered fear to some degree. You'll be able to move forward. You won't be stuck on the hypothetical uncertainties of life.

Many people say that fear is false evidence appearing real (F.E.A.R.). I disagree. Fear is *real*. It's a real feeling. It's a real challenge. Something happens in our physical bodies when fear arises. But this book will serve as a tool and guide to working through the fear factor, no matter what you're afraid of. Open your mind. Open your heart.

> "*Everything you want is on the other side of fear.*"
> —GEORGE ADDAIR

Get to the Root

For God has not given us a spirit of fear,
but of power and of love and of a sound mind.
—2 TIMOTHY 1:7 (NKJV)

*E*very plant has a root. Although we see green trees, plants and flowers sprout up beautifully, there is something happening underground. The root is what supports the plant or tree. It's what nourishes the plant. Without a root, a plant, a flower or a tree cannot grow. It's amazing that what we don't see happening underground is the very thing that's supporting the growth and cultivation of what we see with the natural eye.

Fear is no different. It has a root. It wasn't until I was married that I realized the reason I run away from dogs (even small ones) is because I was attacked by a dog as a child. So now, when even the smallest dog jumps on me, or walks by to sniff me, I am frantic. I never learned how to swim. So, even though I love water parks and my children have a great time, I usually stay in the shallow end. I'm the one who walks around in the lazy river as opposed to floating on a tube because of fear of falling into the water. And while my husband thinks it's quite funny, I don't ride water slides with him for the very reason that he makes me flip into the water just to see me fight my way to the top.

If you watch the news or listen to the radio regularly, you are definitely more apt to develop a spirit of fear. In addition to daily shootings in our neighborhoods, at schools and even churches, now we receive Amber Alerts on our cell phones in the middle of the night. We have to worry about terrorist attacks at every major event we may attend. So besides catching the weather, I chose to stop watching the news. I found myself frantic at the gas station or stoplight, thinking someone was going to rob or carjack me. I was afraid to go to church for a month because of the slew of church shootings across the nation. Before I knew it, I was afraid to leave the house and I was afraid for my children to leave the house. That's *fear*. It stops you from moving forward. It paralyzes your entire life—if you let it. It makes you panic when absolutely nothing has gone wrong. It's the innate reaction to the simple possibility that something, somewhere, is about to go terribly wrong.

In my opinion, many people misinterpret 2 Timothy 1:7. Many believers quote the verse: *For God has not given us a spirit of fear, but of power and of love and of a sound mind.* If we dig deeper into the text, that doesn't mean that fear isn't real or just a figment of our imagination. I'm inclined to believe that although the Bible tells us that God has not given us a spirit of fear, it doesn't tell us the spirit of fear won't come upon us. Fear is very real. It's an authentic feeling that is often accompanied by adverse reactions from the body. Your palms may sweat. Your hands or legs may shake. Your heart may beat faster than normal. Those are all very real, natural reactions to fear—whether it's from an external or internal source.

So, if 2 Timothy 1:7 tells us that *God* has not given us a spirit of fear, we know that it comes from someone or somewhere else. That doesn't mean we won't be fearful. That doesn't mean we won't be scared or timid at times. I interpret the verse as saying even though God does not give us the spirit of fear, we will still experience the spirit of fear. It is simply from the enemy. It's not from God. The enemy knows if he can keep you fearful, he can keep you stagnant. You won't write the book because of fear, but the root cause is that teacher who told you in second grade that you weren't a good writer. You won't start the business because of fear, but the root cause is really the business that failed when you were fresh out of college. Instead of driving, you'd much rather catch the bus or subway out of fear when, in reality, you're still shaken up from the time you had that bad accident.

Every ounce of fear has a root. It has a foundation. Many times, what we see on the surface looks nothing like the root. We put imaginary walls up because of fear of another friend or loved one hurting us even worse than the residual pain we have left. Many women fear dating because they think all men only want one thing. I've even heard women say, "All men cheat at some point." Others have said, "All the good men are already married." Generalization will surely lead to frustration. For the women who think this way, who speak this way, there is a root. That root is hurt. It's bitterness and brokenness. And until those women deal with the root cause, not only will they remain stagnant in their dating life—but they will continue to subconsciously attract men who cheat. After all, Proverbs 18:21 tells us, *The tongue can bring death or life; those who love to talk will reap the consequences.* So, while we shape our very own futures with our words, the root of fear will cause us to think, speak and, thus, experience continual defeat.

Just like a gardener must pull up the ground to plant or pull up the roots, we must pull up the root of fear. If we don't pull up weeds by the root, they simply grow back later. In the same way, when we deal with things on the surface only, we don't deal with the root cause. We simply eliminate temporary symptoms or effects. But something is lying beneath that's causing what we see on the surface. It may be the death of a child or parent. It could be that hurtful divorce that changed your whole mindset about men. Maybe you grew up in poverty and now, every time you get money, you spend it because no one taught you how to properly manage your finances. Perhaps you don't trust women who try to befriend you because your best friend betrayed you.

Ask God to show you the root. Ask Him to show you how to break up that ground in your heart. It's preventing you from moving forward in your destiny assignment. Sure, you may experience some growth and monumental success. But anything that's tied to a root can only grow so far. A tree can only grow up and out so much. It's confined to the space where it's planted because it is attached to the ground by the root. Trees spread their roots deep and wide, and uprooting breaks several of their roots. Not all uprooted trees can be saved, but in some cases, you may successfully revive the tree by replanting it.

It's time to uproot and get replanted!

IN THE FACE OF FEAR
Checkpoint

1. What are you attached to that won't allow you to grow?

   _____

   _____

   _____

   _____

   _____

2. Who are you connected to that won't let you grow beyond their level of success and/or their perceived notion of who you are?

   _____

   _____

   _____

   _____

   _____

3. Search your heart for the root of bitterness and unforgiveness. Who do you need to write a letter to or have a conversation with to pluck it up by the root?

_____

_____

_____

_____

_____

_____

4. What's the worst thing that you perceive can happen to you in life?

_____

_____

_____

_____

_____

_____

5. What is your greatest fear, and what do you need to do to overcome the fear factor in that area?

_____

_____

_____

_____

_____

The Rear-View Mirror

*W*hen I was a little girl, I had a children's Bible with illustrations. While this Bible didn't include every story of the Bible, it highlighted some of the key stories in the Word. In addition to the story of Adam and Eve, the birth of Jesus and His crucifixion on the cross, my favorite Bible story was the story of Lot and his wife. In Genesis 19, two angels met Lot at the city gate. When Lot insisted that the angels stay at his home, he probably didn't know that the men of Sodom would come to "have their way" with the two men. Lot even suggested that the men of Sodom take his daughters, who were still virgins, and have their way with them. They declined his offer. That's where the story takes a dramatic turn. The two men urged Lot to gather all his relatives in the city and to flee. They informed Lot in advance that they were there to destroy the city. Even though Lot warned his daughters' fiancés, they took it as a joke and stayed behind.

The angels told Lot to hurry, but the Word tells us that he dragged his feet. He was moving slowly. Maybe he was stalling to give his relatives another chance to join him in the journey. Maybe he thought if he stayed longer, the angels wouldn't destroy the city. Nonetheless, the angels literally grabbed his arms, and the arms of his wife and daughters and put them safely outside the city. Then, the angels instructed Lot and his family to run for their lives. They told them not to look back or stop anywhere on the way. As soon as Lot was safely in the town of Zoar, God rained down fire and brimstone on Sodom and Gomorrah, destroying everything and everyone in the city. The next thing that happened in the story is what always fascinated me so much as a child.

Genesis 19:26 says, *But Lot's wife looked back and turned into a pillar of salt.* In my children's Bible, Lot's wife simply looked like a statue. She was frozen in her stance, covered in salt. In her disobedience to the word of the angels, she chose to look back. There was nothing to return to. Nothing to look forward to going back to. The entire city and its inhabitants were destroyed. Yet, she made a deliberate choice to look back. I always made my grandmother read this Bible story to me out loud. It was funny in a way—almost intriguing—that this woman, simply by turning around and looking back, turned to a pillar of salt and died.

It wasn't until I was well into my 30s that I understood why that story has always been my favorite Bible story. I was sitting in a service when the Holy Spirit spoke to me ever so clearly: "The reason you love the story of Lot's wife so much is because you always look back." Stunned, almost ashamed, I had to stop and analyze what the Holy Spirit was saying. In friendships, more than any other relationships, I always *look back*. I'm the person who tries to still maintain friendships from high school and college. I call and text people who haven't texted or called me in months. I reach out just to say, "I love you!" I shoot a text just to say, "I miss you." I'm inclined to go to birthday celebrations and events of friends I haven't talked to in years. It's almost like an obligation.

So, when the Holy Spirit brought this to my attention, I had to pause. At that moment, the Holy Spirit told me something so simple, yet profound: "Stop calling and texting, and see how long it takes them to call or text you." As hurtful as it was, many of them never called. They never texted just to see how I was doing. I hardly ever get the text that says, "Hey! Just want you to know I love you and miss you!" It hit me like a ton of bricks, but it was the reality check I needed to move forward—and not look back.

There's a reason that the rear-view mirror of a vehicle is smaller than the windshield. When you drive, you spend much more time looking through the windshield, moving forward, than you do looking in the rear-view mirror. Unless you're backing out of a parking spot, parallel parking, or using it as a mirror to quickly apply last-minute lipstick, you don't look in the rear-view mirror. While the rear-view mirror is there for safety reasons, there is much more at stake regarding your safety if you don't look through the windshield while you're driving. When you're moving forward, what's in front of you is much more important than what is behind you. As it relates to friendships, I was always reaching back. Always trying to pull others up and along the journey with me. Always looking back to old friends and acquaintances to celebrate my successes. At my book launch celebrations and special events, I've always looked at the door in anticipation that the one friend I love dearly, who lives out of state, will surprise me and show up—*just for me*. While some long-time friends have surprised me over the years, more often than not, the people I expected to show never showed. So, I learned to celebrate the people who did show up. The people who came and said, "Congratulations! I'm so proud of you." The people who bought not one, but five books and gave them away as gifts. The people who couldn't purchase a book showed up anyway to put $3 in my hands and hug me because, the reality is, it was all they had.

Ironically, the people who continue to show up the most are those I don't know personally. I don't know them deeply. They may follow my posts on social media or may have met me one time at an event for writers. But, most times, when people come to the table to purchase a book, their names escape me. I may know their faces, but I couldn't tell you their names if you paid me $1,000. But they're present. They come to celebrate my accomplishment, to celebrate me. They're front and center, clapping and cheering. And the people I've known for years are generally nowhere to be found. Untouchable.

Life is fluid. It changes and transforms. It's not a straight journey that's void of speed bumps or potholes. More times than not, it's a winding road. It's intentionally set up with hills and valleys, potholes and smooth terrain. Even if you drive on a freeway daily, and you know the exits and how many lanes the freeway has, the day that road crews go to work to fix the potholes is the day that you have to find a detour. Many times, we look back because it's what's familiar. We're comfortable with the familiar. We know certain friends. We're content in certain relationships. Even if the relationship is broken and doesn't add much value to our lives, we know what we're going to get in that relationship. Fear sets in when we don't know what a new friendship, or a new relationship, will look like. Can you be yourself? Will they criticize you? Will they notice your flaws and pull away suddenly, leaving you to do life alone?

People become our crutches. When I was going through a rough patch in my marriage, I took my two children and stayed with one of my friends and her family. We stayed with her a week and a half before I went home. She was my escape. She was my way out. When my husband and I got into an argument, and decided that we once again wanted a divorce, I'd move in with her temporarily. She never turned me away. She never told me to go home to my husband. Her door was always open to me and the children. Finally, after two years of many tumultuous times in the marriage, she informed me that she and her family were moving to Atlanta. I was happy for her, but deep down inside, there was a piece of me that wondered, "Now what? Whose house will I stay at if I have another argument with my husband and I decide to leave?" It was a selfish thought, but I had an emotional meltdown.

When my friend and her family moved, I didn't go say, "Goodbye." I didn't go to help them pack. I wasn't totally in agreement with them moving, but I knew they had to go. I didn't realize it then, but over time, it was crystal clear that she was my *crutch*. I didn't have to seek God. I didn't pray often. I didn't seek counseling. I didn't have to because I knew her home—she—was my place of escape. She was my way out. And in a weekend, that blanket of comfort was removed. For years, I thought she'd fly in for my book launch. She'd surprise me for my first conference. She'd hop on a plane for my dad's memorial service. But she never walked through the door.

I was familiar with her. I'd poured out my heart to her. She knew all the deep secrets and the history of my husband, my home, my life. However, what I've learned over time is that anything, anyone we replace with God, anything we exalt above our relationship with Him, He will remove. I had to learn to let go. To cut the cord. Many times, we hold onto things, people and places because it's all we've known. It's where we settle. But when the time comes to be uprooted from the place of familiarity, and God charges us to move forward, we can't reach back.

We can't keep turning around. We can't take five steps forward, then three steps back. It's fear of the unknown. But when you take a road trip, even if you run into rain or a snowstorm, you know you're too far away from your original destination to turn around and go back home. You may move slowly. You may pull over to rest. You may even turn your brights on to see the road better. But you're focused on what's in full view of the windshield, not what's in the rear-view mirror. Because when you're driving, especially in a storm, one second that you take to look back in the rear-view mirror, the one second you take your eyes off the road ahead, could mean disaster.

It may be a relationship with an old fling. It may be a friend from college. It may even be a family member who you promised to look after when his or her parents passed away. I challenge you to do what the Holy Spirit challenged me to do. Stop calling. Stop texting. Stop going out of your way to do what works for them if they never reciprocate the relationship. You can't be in a relationship by yourself. There is so much more ahead of you than what is behind you. Keep moving. Move forward. Don't look back. Don't pull back. Take a lesson from Lot's wife. Looking back, even for a moment, could lead to death.

IN THE FACE OF FEAR
Checkpoint

1. What names and numbers do you need to remove from your cell phone in order to move forward?

   _____

   _____

   _____

   _____

   _____

2. Who (or what) have you placed more value on than your relationship with God?

   _____

   _____

   _____

   _____

   _____

3. What type of people do you need to connect with as you move forward to gain greater momentum?

___

___

___

___

___

___

4. How does your relationship with your family and/or friends prevent you from moving forward totally?

___

___

___

___

___

___

5. What is your greatest fear as it relates to moving forward without certain people in your life?

_____

_____

_____

_____

_____

_____

_____

Accountability Partners

Year after year, people around the world make New Year's resolutions. It may be to eat healthier and exercise daily. Some people set out to kick-start their business at the beginning of the new year. Others set out to complete a book or travel overseas for the first time. In most recent years, many people even create vision boards to remind them of their goals for the year. A vision board is generally a poster board that has pictures and words (sometimes cut out of magazines) that represent what a person wants to accomplish. It's what they're believing for. It's what they plan to complete. Habakkuk 2:2 says, *Then the Lord answered me and said:*

> *"Write the vision*
> *And make it plain on tablets,*
> *That he may run who reads it.*
> *For the vision is yet for an appointed time;*
> *But at the end it will speak, and it will not lie.*
> *Though it tarries, wait for it;*
> *Because it will surely come,*
> *It will not tarry."*

While we no longer write on tablets of stone, we write with pen and paper, or we create a visual picture as a reminder of the promise. While writing ourselves a note or taking time to cut out hundreds of pictures and words to create a collage to remind us of what we said we'd accomplish, many times, that is not enough accountability. When we're not accountable to anyone, no one knows what we're working on. Nobody else knows the self-imposed deadlines that we've missed. Some people intentionally don't have accountability because, deep down, they know their goals are farfetched or they've set goals they don't really want to accomplish.

Setting a goal to lose weight is a great goal to have. Annually, gym memberships skyrocket in January. But oftentimes, by March or April, many of those people who frequented the gym in the beginning of the year end up simply paying monthly for a service they don't take full advantage of. The people who are most successful at weight loss are not those who spend two or three hours in the gym daily. It's the people who have accountability. They hire a personal trainer, which is often not included in the price of a general gym membership. They get up at 5 a.m. daily to run by the water with a friend who is also committed to losing weight. Some people even do weekly weigh-ins at the gym, where the trainer or instructor analyzes their weight loss. When people have a genuine desire to lose weight, and keep the weight off, it becomes a lifestyle change—not just something they do at the beginning of the year.

Many people don't like the word "accountability." It sounds stern, stoic, and almost militant to some. Some people see accountability as a form of control and ruling. While children know that they must obey their parents, many adults follow the mantra, "I'm grown, and no one can tell me what to do!" That's true—to a certain extent. Life is full of distractions. Life is what happens to us when we're in the midst of pursuing our dreams and we hit a roadblock or construction, making us come to a standstill in the process. You set a goal with tangible deliverables and dates; however, a year later, you're no closer to completing that goal than when you started. What happened? Life.

We lose time due to sickness or accidents. We get tired or sleepy after work, so we just go to bed. We keep putting it off until tomorrow, and tomorrow turns into seven years. We experience the loss of family members and friends. Our children need us to attend that field trip, that PTA meeting or that classroom party. The only way we are sure to get back on track, the only way many will ever make it to the finish line of any project, is to have an accountability partner.

While this person may get on your nerves or irritate you daily, they are there for your benefit. Once you share a dream or goal with someone else, they become your cheerleader. They become your pusher and your checker. Some days, you will love them. Other days, not so much. Either way, you need them in your life. You need this person to ask you every so often, "How's the book coming along? Is there anything I can do to help you jumpstart the business? What day is your launch party?" This is the person who won't let you forget about the dream, the goal, the wish *you said* you wanted to accomplish. This person will stay on your head about it until you finally buckle down and get it done.

Having a big dream is great. Having faith in God is phenomenal. But faith without works is dead. I don't care how much faith you have or how many positive affirmations you speak daily. Until you move into action and implementation, you won't see any manifestation of the promise. Without the process, there is no promise.

And, let's be clear. You may need a different accountability partner for every area of your life. When I'm writing books, I have one set of accountability partners. When I get serious about fasting from fried chicken (which is not often), I use my husband as my accountability partner. He's been in the United States Marine Corps and he's just as militant when it comes to fasting and healthy food choices. When I'm planning a writers' conference or workshop, I tell four or five of my friends who are publishers and/or authors because I know they will continually ask me about the event date, time and place until I post the flyer on social media. I make it a point to surround myself with people who won't let me off the hook. They won't let me be tired or sick for too many days at a time without producing something toward my goals. They call me. They come over. When we go out for lunch or dinner, I don't get up from the table without them asking me about my dreams, goals and visions.

Your accountability partners are there when you want to give up and give in. They help you keep going when you feel like you can't take another step toward your goal. When things seem impossible, they encourage you and affirm you—helping you to cross the finish line and even celebrate afterward. When someone is constantly pushing you and asking about the latest, greatest masterpiece that you're producing, there is no room and no time for fear. Accountability helps you complete the task—*even if you're scared.*

IN THE FACE OF FEAR
Checkpoint

1. List two key people who can serve as accountability partners in your business/ministry.

   _____

   _____

   _____

   _____

2. List two key people who can serve as accountability partners in your personal or family goals.

   _____

   _____

   _____

   _____

3. How often will you connect with your accountability partners?

_____

_____

_____

_____

_____

_____

_____

4. In what way can you serve as an accountability partner for other friends and/or family members?

_____

_____

_____

_____

_____

_____

_____

5. How has your mindset changed regarding accountability since reading this chapter?

_____

_____

_____

_____

_____

_____

_____

Plan & Practice

Benjamin Franklin said, "If you fail to plan, you are planning to fail!" While many people know this famous quote, very few actually implement it. In essence, what Benjamin Franklin was saying is that, without a plan of action, one is bound to fail. That doesn't just apply to business or entrepreneurship. It applies to finances. It applies to marriage. It applies to building a new structure and even demolishing an old one. Without a plan, preferably a written plan, failure is inevitable.

If you don't have a plan, you can't measure success (or lack thereof). When someone gets serious about losing weight, they don't just go to the gym when they feel like it. They schedule their workout times, but they also plan their meals. They have a strategy and a plan to get to their desired goal. If you are hosting a conference, you ideally have a written plan with steps and deliverables that, many times, are *due* even after the conference has taken place. When you don't plan, the event is bound to go haywire. You won't accomplish your weight loss goals. You'll be at next year's

New Year's Eve party talking about the same goal, without any tangible results or movement.

When my daughter got her first bike, it had training wheels. While she was excited about riding in the driveway, and eventually the neighborhood, what she didn't realize was that the training wheels were really balancing her and preventing her from falling over. She didn't have to do much work to balance the bike; all she had to do was pedal forward. However, when she got her second bike, it was clear that she needed more *practice*. She realized that she no longer had the training wheels to help her balance and she had to do more work. After practicing for a while, she realized that she had to learn to balance while she pedaled. It has been said that once you learn to ride a bike, you'll never forget how to ride. People often use the analogy, "It's just like riding a bike!" when explaining to someone that there are certain things you just won't forget how to do.

Working in corporate America was my training wheels for entrepreneurship. I wrote for several corporate communications departments at many *Fortune 500* companies, and earned several awards, cars and bonuses for my hard work. Looking back on it now, besides my tenure at AT&T Yellow Pages for six years, I didn't work at any corporate job for longer than two years. It was almost like I was there to learn what I needed to learn. When it was time to go, I was laid off or I found a better opportunity and moved on. I didn't know it then, but my training on the job at Chariton Valley answering service and the OnStar call center was preparation for how to properly deal with difficult customers in my own business. Those positions taught me that the customer is always right (yes, even when they're wrong). Because those companies valued customer retention, pleasing even the most difficult customers was key to their business model. If nothing else, those jobs taught me patience when dealing with people of all backgrounds, in all types of business transactions.

During my tenure at AT&T Yellow Pages, I learned how to perfect my craft of proofreading, editing and quality assurance as a whole. Since I was responsible for editing ads for businesses within the Yellow Pages before the books went to print, I knew I had to be meticulous and careful about my work. Whenever a mistake was printed in an ad in the books, the company lost money and had to compensate the customer financially, as well as with an extension on their ad campaign. If I overlooked one misspelled word, an incorrect website or one wrong number in a phone number, it could cost the company thousands of dollars. This position taught me the importance of not only editing and proofreading multiple times, but also the importance of having multiple people review the same document. Each editor and proofreader always found something different.

When I transitioned to DTE Energy, Detroit's light and gas conglomerate, I had the opportunity to improve my overall writing and interviewing skills. Not only did I have to write three articles per week for the intranet, but I also had to interview employees in different departments and network with people I did not know—from janitors to executives. In this position, I gained a greater confidence in asking those questions that could've made the interviewee uncomfortable. I gained a greater respect for news reporters. While I had a deep love for writing, I soon realized that I strongly disliked the news interviewing process. I just wanted to write and edit.

I was also exposed to broadcast journalism, something in which I was never exposed to while I was in college. As a communications consultant, I was responsible for writing the content for many safety videos, going in the field to interview employees in their work environments and reviewing final video edits for approval. While I enjoyed the video shoots and the onsite interactions, I realized that I'd much rather be behind a computer, writing the story behind the scenes.

It was when I landed what I thought was my dream job that my eyes were truly opened to my purpose and passion. I took a position as a content editor at McCann Erickson, a worldwide marketing and ad agency. When I came on the scene, there were only three other editors on the team supporting more than fifty account directors. In addition to a full benefits package and my own office, the company also offered all employees free wine and beer on Fridays at 4 p.m. We had an onsite popcorn machine and, almost every day, there was some form of catering or gathering with food. This was the life—or so I thought.

What I soon realized during my time at McCann is that working an 11 a.m. to 7 p.m. shift doesn't leave much family time once you get home. I never saw my husband and children, including my newborn baby. I never had date nights with my husband because, by the time I got home at 8 p.m., he was oftentimes preparing the children and himself for bed. This was when I also realized that $45,000 a year wasn't as much money as I thought it was. In addition, I learned that money truly isn't everything. While I enjoyed the job, and I enjoyed having a private office and free lunches, the sacrifice for it all was my family. I wasn't willing to pay that cost long-term. As hard as it was to stop working full-time and transition back into contract work, I knew I had to move into something else for the betterment of my family and my marriage.

I interviewed with *The Michigan Chronicle*, Detroit's African American newspaper, for an editorial director position. I didn't interview once or twice. I went in three times, only to be denied the position because the paper couldn't meet my salary requirements. I was devastated. The same day that I got the rejection from *The Michigan Chronicle*, however, I received a call for an interview at Mercedes-Benz Financial Services. I interviewed for the position of internal communications consultant for the IT department and, no sooner than I was out the door and into my car, my phone rang from my contract house to inform me that the company wanted to offer me the position. I didn't understand it then, but I do now. When one door closes, another one is sure to open. It may not open right away. It may not open the same day. But it's definitely a redirection to something that is oftentimes much better.

During my time at Mercedes-Benz Financial Services, I gained global communications experience. I was responsible for writing the U.S. and Germany communications for the IT team that needed to go out to the entire employee population. I reported directly to the Chief Information Officer for Mercedes-Benz, who was German. Not only was I responsible for writing his communications to the department, other leaders and the enterprise as a whole, but I managed his LinkedIn profile and revamped his professional bio and resume often. Because he spoke on many platforms often, he would often ask me to create talking points for his speeches. We would review them together to ensure they contained the gist of his messages and overall voice. In essence, this position honed my skills as a ghostwriter.

Because many of the employees were of German or Arabic descent, their English translation was oftentimes broken or inaccurate. So, when someone in the department needed to send out professional communications, I was the go-to. And, unlike other positions, I was now responsible for supporting senior managers, supervisors, and managers with their communications, in addition to the general communications for the department news. I was required to not only write on a more professional level but also in a way that was engaging for the employee population. This was the place where my writing was stretched to new levels.

By now, you get that practice isn't optional. If you're going to become a master of anything, you have to practice it almost daily. Some people say, "If you don't use it, you lose it." I don't necessarily subscribe to that way of thinking. I believe if the gift and seed of passion is planted within, whenever it is watered and cultivated, it will grow. While I know there are many untapped dreams and visions in the grave today, I believe that as long as you still have breath in your body, you still have time to create a plan, practice and walk into your passion and purpose.

Of course, now that I'm a full-time entrepreneur, I can look back at each season in my life and see the role it played in preparing me for where I am today. More often than not, as a full-time entrepreneur, I plan my year in advance. It's not enough to plan for the week or the month. I plan my events sometimes a year in advance. I already know where I'm hosting next year's writers' conference and what places we want to travel to next year as a family. While other opportunities will come, and other doors will open, I continue to plan my life and business to the best of my ability. I also decided to be a lifetime student. Even though I've been writing and editing for over twenty years, there are still things I can learn about writing in different genres, writing for various audiences and even how to transform my writing since I am now more mature. If you're going to master your craft, you've got to plan and practice, over and over again.

IN THE FACE OF FEAR
Checkpoint

1. Write out a 30-day plan for your social media promotions.

   _____
   _____
   _____
   _____
   _____
   _____

2. List the days and times of the week you will practice enhancing your craft.

   _____
   _____
   _____
   _____
   _____

3. Who do you need to connect with in this season who can help you plan and practice effectively?

_____

_____

_____

_____

_____

_____

_____

4. How far in advance do you plan for your business/ministry? How can you better improve the plan?

_____

_____

_____

_____

_____

_____

_____

5. How has your mindset changed regarding planning and practice since reading this chapter?

_____

_____

_____

_____

_____

_____

_____

In the Shadows

Generally, when you hear someone referring to a shadow, it has a negative connotation. We may tell our children that they don't have to live in the shadows of their siblings or remind friends and colleagues to not live in the shadow of their past. The Word of God even speaks about "the valley of the shadow of death," which, for many people, has a negative meaning. However, I see great benefits in living in the shadows of others. But it depends on who it is, of course.

When I worked in customer service for OnStar, training was anywhere from four to six weeks. Once I completed my classroom training, I moved into on-the-job training. But, because I was new to the company, its products and services, and even the computer system, I was paired with a more seasoned employee until I got the hang of things. The company called this "job shadowing." For the first week or two on the job, I simply watched the person I was shadowing. I listened to how she took calls. I watched how she handled irate customers in a professional manner, even though they screamed and cursed at her. I listened to the verbiage she used when she spoke to customers and dealers alike. For some calls, there was a script. But, in some instances, she had to resolve the concern with her general knowledge of the products and services. She was also wise enough to know that, if for some reason she couldn't resolve the customer's concern, she had to get a supervisor on the phone with the customer. We called that *escalation*. She knew what she could, and could not, handle.

Eventually, that shadowing process included me switching seats with her. Even though she was right by my side and could hear my entire conversation with customers through a headset, I was in the driver's seat. However, I didn't have as much fear as I would have had if I had started taking calls alone on the first day of the job. She also had a mute button at her fingertips, so if the customer asked a question and I wasn't sure how to answer it, she could mute our headsets to tell me how to answer and then unmute me to respond to the customer. After every call, she took the time to give me feedback on how I could have handled the previous call differently to maximize the customer's positive experience. After six weeks, I was trained and wise enough to take calls alone about the products and services. For that position, I had graduated from shadowing.

Entrepreneurship is no different. If you're going to be successful as an entrepreneur, you must shadow those people you admire over and over again—until you get to where they are in their career. In the beginning, this was somewhat challenging for me. No one in my family had ever worked as full-time entrepreneurs (unless you count the drug dealers as entrepreneurs).

I was taught and raised to go to school, get a degree, work hard in corporate America, and retire from a corporate position by the age of 65. But, after working several contract jobs, and getting laid off time and time again when a company decided to downsize, that plan didn't seem promising for me.

When I was laid off for the third and final time from Raytheon, I knew this was *it*. I didn't want to look for a new job. I didn't want to go through several interviews at one company, only to later be denied the opportunity because the company couldn't meet my salary requirements. It had to work this time. My business had to work. There were no other options. I had to use what was in my hands to feed my family, to fund my dreams and to merely survive. I could no longer depend on an outside force to supply my family's needs. It was too inconsistent for me. My nerves were bad. My anxiety was at an all-time high. I had to find some sense of stability. And as unstable as entrepreneurship can be, it was the most stable option for me at the time. So, I had to make the cut from corporate to full-time creative. But who do you shadow when you're a full-time entrepreneur?

Other full-time entrepreneurs.

I knew several, but their work and journey became magnified to me once I "lost my job" for the last time. While the first couple of months were rocky and almost depressing, I eventually pulled myself up by the bootstraps and connected with like-minded individuals who were already on the road I was now attempting to navigate. Even though most of my friends are full-time speakers, coaches, graphic designers and publishers, the concept remains the same—get paid (and well) for solving a problem. So, I had to have conversations with those entrepreneurs about marketing, selling, and promoting my business and my personal brand. In addition, I had to shadow other business owners. In the process, I learned that I always need to get a deposit for every service or product—if not the full amount—upfront. At first, I feared that no one would give me a deposit and I hadn't done any work yet. Wrong! I was the only one left holding a finished product, waiting on a client to pay me when they were ready to pay me.

I also had to set boundaries. Some clients wanted to call me at 10 p.m. about their manuscript. If I was working in corporate America, no one would call my office phone at

10 p.m. because they know I'm probably not available. Yet, as an entrepreneur, consumers assume that we work around the clock and we're up at midnight working on projects. That's not always the case. I had to set specific work hours daily and specific times when I would (and would not) answer my phone or respond to text messages from clients. I had to set certain days and times in which I could meet clients for coffee or breakfast. I wasn't available at the drop of a dime for every client who called and said they wanted to meet me in person in the middle of the day. I had to set solid, clear boundaries or customers were going to walk all over me and my family. They didn't care about my schedule and family until I made it clear that those things were my priority.

More than anything, I learned how to treat small business owners and entrepreneurs since I was now in a full-time role as just that. I learned how to value and respect their time and energy. I learned how to effectively barter with other entrepreneurs, when applicable. Now, this was not always my go-to strategy when I wanted to get something done, but I knew I offered a stellar service and product that most of the people I'm connected to needed or wanted. So, bartering has always been an option for me. However, it may not be an option for all business owners. It must be mutually beneficial.

By now, you get the point. Connect with like-minded individuals who are already where you are trying to go in business. Shadow those people in your field, or even general entrepreneurs, so you can get the gist of what full-time entrepreneurship looks like day to day. Don't just shadow people once, either. Sometimes, you may have to shadow someone in your field for months. Even at different intervals in your business, you may have to shadow different professionals for different reasons. But find someone who has some lasting, excellent results in whatever it is that they do—and shadow them.

IN THE FACE OF FEAR
Checkpoint

1. Where do you need to network to maximize your exposure to full-time, successful entrepreneurs?

   _____

   _____

   _____

   _____

   _____

2. What fears do you have about shadowing another entrepreneur?

   _____

   _____

   _____

   _____

   _____

3. What areas of your business could most benefit from one-on-one feedback from other entrepreneurs?

_____

_____

_____

_____

_____

_____

4. What top three questions would you ask an entrepreneur on the first day you shadow them?

_____

_____

_____

_____

_____

_____

5. How has your mindset changed regarding "living in the shadows of others" since reading this chapter?

_____

_____

_____

_____

_____

_____

Prayer

*I*saiah 26:3 (WEB) says, *You will keep [him] in perfect peace, [whose] mind [is] stayed [on you]; because he trusts in you.* When I was laid off from my last corporate position, I immediately went into a state of fear and anxiety. Even though I had my business for seven years on the side, I wasn't certain what running a business full-time would look like. I was so used to getting up in the morning, driving to an office, and waiting on work and instructions to be handed to me. Now, I was not only in charge of the business side of things, but the tactical assignments as well. I was more afraid of failing than succeeding. Even with both a bachelor's and master's degree, somehow, I felt unqualified. Those degrees helped me succeed in corporate America, but college taught me nothing about being an entrepreneur. My entire college experience was centered on finding a great job in my field, working to climb the corporate ladder and retiring at the age of 65. It didn't take long for me to realize that wouldn't be my narrative.

I attended church often and I was saved. I believed in Jesus Christ and I trusted Him with my whole heart. However, the first month after the layoff, I fell into a deep depression. I'd just completed my first stage play, *When the Smoke Clears*, which is based off my bestselling book. I had three sold-out shows downtown Detroit that weekend and I didn't just break even; I made a few thousand dollars. Yet, the morning after, I felt as though I'd hit a plateau in my career and in life.

That Monday, as I sat on the couch watching TV, I was lost. Destitute. Loopy. I almost had an out-of-body experience. I could feel pressure weighing on my shoulders. I could feel darkness staring me in the face. I didn't know what to do next and, honestly, I wasn't sure there was a next. I wanted to kill myself. I hadn't had bouts of depression and suicidal thoughts since I was a teenager, so this struck me in the head like a lightning bolt. I couldn't see my way out of the dark hole. I read my Word, but it didn't seem to shift my mindset. It didn't seem like it was penetrating my soul. I listened to worship music and felt absolutely nothing. I didn't know *what*, or *who*, changed me. But I knew something was wrong with me and I needed help.

I contemplated checking myself into a mental hospital or transitional home. I didn't feel safe around my husband and children because I didn't want them to see me hurt myself.

Of course, I didn't want to hurt them either. I lost my desire for writing and editing. I still had to work on clients' projects, but I was only operating at 47% of my normal capacity. It was as if the enemy was saying to me, "This is it. You're done. You won't do anything greater. This is the end for you, and you should just kill yourself. God won't use you anymore. He's done all He is going to do." But somewhere deep down in my soul, I knew those statements were lies. I knew that God loved me, and I knew that if I still had breath in my body, His purpose was not yet complete in my life. After about 45 days of "walking around in a spiritual wilderness," I went to a church service at Increasing Faith Ministries. Pastor Tammy Stephens prayed for me at the altar, and her specific words were: "You shall live and not die! You have greater works to do!"

In that moment, something broke. The firm grip holding me hostage relaxed and the darkness lifted. As the days passed, I continued to feel stronger and stronger. I regained my passion for writing and editing, and I felt like I could produce excellence for my clients once again. The weight of the darkness that surrounded me kept me from praying for myself. I didn't know what to say. I didn't know who I could trust to pray for me, who I could tell I was battling suicidal thoughts without them turning me in to the nearest psychiatric ward. During that time, as I slowly rose from the pit of darkness, I heard God's voice so clearly say, "Take it one day at a time. I'll tell you what to do. One step at a time. Just trust Me to tell you what to do daily." And since then, I've done just that. I didn't have many models for what successful entrepreneurship looks like, so I listened to the voice of Holy Spirit daily, almost hourly even. Otherwise, I found myself wasting days by sleeping, watching TV and playing on social media. I knew that wasn't God's plan for my life or my business. I had to learn how to be CEO, employee and employer. I didn't have time to waste.

Today, I pray over my business daily. I speak positive declarations over my family, my business and my home. Daily, I say, "Father God, I thank you that I make no less than $XXXX a week in my business." As I grow and progress, that number changes. At one point, I prayed to make no less than $2,000 a week in my business. Then, $3,000 a week. And as I continue to increase in skillset, service offerings and excellence, that number increases. Fill in that number with whatever your number is for the week. Ask God for a specific target amount weekly, whether it's the number of clients you have that week or the amount of money you bring in. But remember that faith without works is dead. God may send you the money in the form of work. So, you may have to work for ten clients that week to get the amount of money you were believing God for. Unfortunately, many of us miss the answer to our prayers and the blessings because the answer comes in the form of work. Most people don't want to work harder. They want to be on a beach, sipping a tasty alcoholic beverage, while clients flood their PayPal account with money. Anything is possible, but until you've been in business for a significant number of years, you won't be able to benefit from those types of systems.

Pray that God will grant you wisdom beyond your years. When you're a full-time entrepreneur, you're going to have to learn how to serve various types of clientele. You also need to be clear about who your customer is and is not. Not everyone can be your customer. Whether it's because they can't afford your products or services, or they are working on something that doesn't line up with your values and ethics, you're going to have to know when to bow out of a deal. All money isn't good money. Be intentional and strategic about the projects you take on and the clients you serve.

Pray about your prices. Even though you should conduct your share of market research to determine what others in your industry are charging, that doesn't mean you have to price your products or services at the exact same prices as the competition. Know what you bring to the table and charge accordingly, plus tax! When I started my editing service, I charged $2 and $3 per page. Today, that rate has risen to $5 and $7 per page. However, it took me seven years to get to that point. Again—use wisdom. You don't want to underbid yourself, but you don't want to overcharge either. No other entrepreneur can tell you what to charge. You must do your research and be led by Holy Spirit. In the end, we're in business for ourselves as entrepreneurs. But we're in business to fund the Kingdom. Our businesses belong to God.

Finally, pray the Word over your business. Pick Scriptures that resonate with where you are in your business and make those your daily confessions. For example, you could say, "Father God, I thank you that I am the head and not the tail. Thank you that I am above, not beneath." That faith confession is based on Deuteronomy 28:13. When you pray the Word of God over your business, not only do you remind God of His promises to His people—but you get into covenant agreement with the Word. The Word of God also teaches us that there is power in the tongue. We have the power to build or tear down with our words. So, make a distinct choice to speak words that build your business, not words that tear it down. You can say something like, "Father God, I thank you that you are sending me quality clientele who value my products and services, and don't mind paying my prices. Thank you, Lord, that you are showing me favor with man and God. Thank you, Father God, that there are men and women, sitting in boardrooms, discussing my name and strategizing how they can work with me." I've tried it consistently and speaking these things over my business not only changed the trajectory of the level of clientele I attract—but it also further positioned me as an expert in my field, which allows me to increase my pricing without people complaining (most times).

At the time this book was completed, I had only been an entrepreneur for two years. But even in those two years, I can say that I honestly would not have made it as a successful entrepreneur if it wasn't for my prayer life. Not only do my husband and I read the Word of God daily, but we also pray over our businesses daily. Because of my success as an entrepreneur, he also stepped out on faith to start his own consulting business. Today, he still works in corporate America as a manager, but his long-term goal is to consult full-time for corporations under the umbrella of his own business. Call us crazy, but we believe that the results we see today are a direct result of the prayers we've prayed over the years.

Prayer is the key, the secret weapon, to running a successful business. For it to work, one must be consistent, intentional, bold and specific. I never pray, "Father God, any way you bless me, I'll be satisfied." That's too vague for me. I believe God is in the details. I specifically asked God to allow me to write and edit for millionaires, CEOs, leaders in *Fortune 500* companies and political figures. And I believe He will do just that.

IN THE FACE OF FEAR
Checkpoint

1. How often do you pray?

   _____
   _____
   _____
   _____
   _____
   _____

2. How and when do you know if you are praying effectively?

   _____
   _____
   _____
   _____
   _____
   _____

3. What Scriptures resonate with you and your business that you can stand on daily?

_____
_____
_____
_____
_____
_____

4. What other business owners can you connect with in prayer to agree about the success of your businesses?

_____
_____
_____
_____
_____
_____
_____

5. Dream big! What dollar amount do you wish to bring into your business weekly?

_____

_____

_____

_____

_____

_____

_____

Execute

Twice a year, I used to host an annual writers' conference in two cities called *The Red Ink Conference*. For the past five years, writers from across the nation have purchased plane tickets, drove for hours, paid for hotel rooms and partnered with others all for a spot in the room with the movers and shakers of the literary industry. The conference consistently proved to be a fun, exciting time of planning, strategy, and networking. I always received positive feedback from the attendees, as well as the speakers. What started out as just a Detroit conference grew into a national conference and made traction in other major cities across the nation, such as Atlanta and Charlotte. But—I found one problem.

People lack execution.

They pay their monies to register and travel. They take notes diligently and they may even shed a few tears as their eyes are opened to the possibilities of writing their books. They connect with great people in the room who have the knowledge, wisdom and capability to move their projects forward in excellence. We position authors to leave with a professional headshot for their book's back cover and website, and we even work on short professional bios and book synopses. Yet, many of those same people who were excited in the room return to their homes and do absolutely nothing. *Nothing.*

They don't write.

They don't journal.

They don't research.

Many of those same people will return next year, and the year after that, to sit in the room once again amongst the movers and shakers. Maybe they think proximity to powerful people is enough. Maybe they think they'll hear something magical that will get down into the depths of their souls and make them pour out onto the pages in a matter of minutes. Maybe they even believe they will receive a mystical formula to get the book done in a day—without them ever writing a word. The truth is that most people want someone to do the work for them. If nothing else, being a full-time entrepreneur has taught me that if you don't get up and do that work, you won't eat. You won't have seed to sow. You won't have gas in your car. You won't have nice things. And your dreams definitely won't come true!

Daily, I make a conscious choice to execute and get *it* done.

It doesn't matter how I feel or don't feel. Feelings can't play a part in your business. Household bills and emergencies come eventually, no matter how you feel about them. So, as leaders and entrepreneurs, the best thing we can do is prepare our umbrella for the storm that will surely come. For many people, it's not that they don't get started; they simply don't finish. Execution means following through on the goal or assignment—not giving up or giving in right in the middle of a project.

For me to obtain my degrees, I had to complete coursework. For me to complete my first book (and even this book), I had to sit down and write. My other option was to pay thousands of dollars to a ghostwriter to compile the book for me, but that would mean I risk losing my voice as an author. I chose the former. While it may have taken seven months to complete my first book, *100 Words of Encouragement: Tidbits of Inspiration*, it took me almost two years to complete the one you are now reading. I had to walk through execution amid my fears before I could ever help you, the reader, soar amid your fears. Had I failed my classes in college, had I spent days and nights watching TV instead of writing, I wouldn't be where I am today. We all have twenty-four hours in a day. For many of us, eight of those hours are spent sleeping. We've got to make the other sixteen count for something special.

It took me a few months to realize that I spend a significant amount of time on social media, which yields me no new customers, contacts, contracts or money. It's leisurely activity that I participate in throughout the day, all day, every day. Finally, I came to a hard realization; I'm addicted to social media. So, when I really need to complete an assignment or get something done, I must remove the social media apps from my phone. It sounds harsh and extreme, but I must "punish" myself that way because, otherwise, I become so consumed with what others are doing that I forget to execute in my own life! We are intentional about scheduling doctors' appointments. Many of us are intentional about scheduling our dentist appointment every six months. We even take the time to get our car washed after a storm so we're not riding around in a dirty vehicle.

Yet, when it comes to our hopes, dreams and wishes, it seems like "life" always happens. Someone gets sick and needs us to come to the hospital. Our spouse wants us to come to bed early. Our children want extra snacks and a bedtime story before they go to bed. Our friends want our advice on how they should handle their next mid-life crisis. Our church wants us to serve in more areas. Meanwhile, we get further and further away from our individual plans and goals.

Contrary to popular belief, it's okay to decline requests. The world will continue to pull on you, your time and your energy if you allow it. You must be strategic and intentional about scheduling the execution of your vision and goals. Use your Google calendar to schedule tasks and set a reminder for when it's approaching. Turn your phone off for a few hours a day. Decide when you will and won't take phone calls. Even if it's a potential new client, they will leave a voicemail if they're serious about doing business with you. Treat social media like a bonus or reward after you've completed your daily tasks.

Share your goals with your accountability partner so he or she can keep you on your toes. As irritating as it may be, you need someone asking you constantly, "Did you finish your book yet? Did you file your LLC paperwork yet? Did you finish your business taxes yet?" Don't pick a "yes" person. You need a person who won't settle for your excuses that oftentimes keep you stuck in the same place. Surround yourself with people who are not just talking about what they want to do, but who are executing it daily.

Biblically speaking, faith without works is dead. A tree that doesn't bear fruit is worthless. So, if you're still on earth, if you still have breath in your body, you're here on purpose with purpose. Find out what it is and pursue it with everything you've got. No one is going to do the work for you. You're going to have to bear down and push. When I gave birth to my daughter, even though my husband was by my side, and the doctors held my legs and feet, I still had to push. There was only so much they could do to help me give birth. Ultimately, it was up to me to make the final push for the baby to come out. If I didn't push, no matter what the people around me did or did not do, I could have died, or the baby could have died in the birth canal. So, don't let your dream die in the birth canal!

IN THE FACE OF FEAR
Checkpoint

1. What project or product do you need to execute immediately?

   _____

   _____

   _____

   _____

   _____

2. What or who do you need to disconnect from so you can execute more efficiently?

   _____

   _____

   _____

   _____

   _____

3. Once you execute and complete a task or project, what will be your reward?

_____

_____

_____

_____

_____

_____

4. How many lives are at stake if you fail to execute in a timely manner?

_____

_____

_____

_____

_____

_____

5. What do you need to do less of in order to execute projects and goals faster?

_____

_____

_____

_____

_____

_____

"F" the Fear Factor

While I used profanity like a sailor in college, at the request of my husband (and the transformation through the Lord, Jesus Christ), I do my best not to use "those" types of words anymore. But I want you to "F" the fear factor. In this case, "F" stands for face. It sounds simple, yet somewhat dumb, to face your fears. However, the reality is, that may be the quickest way to get over it.

For many years, I was terrified to speak in front of live audiences. I was scared I was going to wet my pants, say a curse word or trip over a random cord on the floor and embarrass myself. None of that ever happened, but I felt like it would when I got up to speak in front of a room of strangers. Even though my palms often dripped with perspiration, I held on to the microphone for dear life until I got into the groove of things. Today, the first five minutes or so of any speech I give can be a bit rocky. First, I must feel the audience out and find where I'm comfortable in the room. I often walk and talk, and I prefer a hand-held mic over a lavalier mic. A few minutes in, I'm relaxed, and I can just be myself. I also engage with the audience, allowing them to become a part of my presentation. That way, all eyes are never just on me for an hour or two. I do my best to make every talk or speech interactive. It helps loosen up the atmosphere of the room, and it gives me time to get the jitters out.

Part of my fear is wanting everything to go well. I want everything to flow perfectly. The truth of the matter is life and mishaps will happen. I have found a creative way to work even those "behind-the-scenes" mishaps into my presentation. I don't have to be perfect, and I make that known to my audiences upfront. Not only does that lighten the room's atmosphere, but it makes me more down-to-earth and relatable to those in the room who may not know me personally. Over time, I've tackled my fright of public speaking by doing just that—*speaking*. Ironically, what I found is that I love it—even more so than writing and editing!

Some level of fear may always be present. We're not perfect and it's okay to let others know. However, we can operate in excellence without perfection. If you're going to overcome your fears, you're simply going to have to "F" the fear factor. Whatever it is that keeps you up at night or causes extreme anxiety to come upon you when you think about it, do more of *that*. I wholeheartedly believe that everything you want is on the other side of fear. How and when you make it to "the other side" is up to you.

About the Author

*A*uthors worldwide write better thanks to editorial guru and authorpreneur, Tenita C. Johnson. Perfecting manuscripts for hundreds of best-selling authors, she's on a mission to end the prominent everyday abuse of the English language and rectify punctuation pet peeves. As the founder and CEO of So It Is Written, Tenita collaborates with industry professionals to take manuscripts to the marketplace, positioning authors for success in the literary world. Well-known by many as a human spell check, noun nerd and grammar police, she proudly wears the badge of honor to correct and serve.

Dubbed the book bully by many, she empowers aspiring authors to write from the editor's point of view to save them time and money in the publishing process. She positions writers as experts in the industry, empowering them to create multiple streams of income from just one book. To connect with Tenita, visit SoItIsWritten.net, TenitaJohnson.com or email info@soitiswritten.net.

About So It Is Written

We help entrepreneurs write the ONE book that will expand their reach and get them to SIX figures in record time! Period!

As the leading content curators for six-figure authorpreneurs and entrepreneurs, So It Is Written is best known for helping them package and leverage their expertise into a bestselling book, which amplifies their brand, accelerates their paydays and attracts bigger opportunities!

Let us help you brand in excellence as an author and entrepreneur so you can develop multiple streams of income from just ONE book! Call us at 313.777.8607 today, or email info@soitiswritten.net for more details about our services. We look forward to working with you to make your project one of excellence!

www.ingramcontent.com/pod-product-compliance
Lightning Source LLC
Chambersburg PA
CBHW062140100526
44589CB00014B/1631